THE
Archive Photographs
SERIES

CHICHESTER
1945-1965

THE
Archive Photographs
SERIES

CHICHESTER
1945-1965

Compiled by
Ken Green and Steve Griffiths

CHALFORD

First published 1998
Copyright © Ken Green and Steve Griffiths, 1998

The Chalford Publishing Company
St Mary's Mill, Chalford,
Stroud, Gloucestershire, GL6 8NX

ISBN 0 7524 1105 5

Typesetting and origination by
The Chalford Publishing Company
Printed in Great Britain by
Bailey Print, Dursley, Gloucestershire

Contents

Introduction   7

1. Shops   9

2. Demolition   15

3. New buildings   23

4. Schools   37

5. Sporting Activities   45

6. The Military   51

7. Royal Occasions   57

8. Somerstown   65

9. Events   71

10. Personalities   99

11. Groups   105

12. Street Scenes   115

Acknowledgements   128

About the Authors

Ken Green was born in Chichester in 1932. He was educated locally, entering Chichester High School in the last year of the war; his interest in the times pictured in this book therefore evokes vivid memories for him. Ken was the founder of the Chichester Local History Society in 1986 and has become known for his books on the city's past, as a contributor to Chichester newspapers, and as a broadcaster on local radio stations.

Steve Griffiths was born in Worcester in 1967. He read History at the University of Sheffield and took a Masters Degree in Archives Administration at the University of Liverpool. Since 1994 he has worked at West Sussex County Record Office, where he is the searchroom archivist and is responsible for the office's photographic holdings. He lives with his wife and small daughter in Brighton.

Introduction

The two decades following the end of the Second World War transformed the lives of most British people. More than 2.5 million men and women had returned to civilian life by 1947, many of them eager to build a new society. The general mood for change was reflected in new social and economic developments. The founding of the National Health Service, the 1944 Education Act and the nationalisation of many industries made an enormous impact. Improvements in living standards were slower to appear. Rationing persisted well into the 1950s and rubble-strewn bomb sites stubbornly remained a feature of most urban landscapes. Slowly, however, new buildings began to rise up and new suburbs were planned to meet the demand for housing. As it entered the 1960s, British society became steadily more affluent, ushering in new and exciting fashions in clothing, entertainment and travel.

All of this was reflected in Chichester, although the city had in one respect been more fortunate than many. Compared to the devastation seen elsewhere, Chichester was relatively untouched by enemy air raids; the 1960s planners had a far greater impact upon the city's landscape than the Luftwaffe. The changes that took place in the post-war years transformed the appearance of the city more significantly than at any other time in its history.

Over half of the pictures in this book are drawn from a collection of about 15,000 images, mainly comprising glass plate negatives, originally taken by Chichester Photographic Services Ltd of Whyke Lane, Chichester. Along with the firm's day books they were given to the West Sussex Record Office when its founder and owner, Harry Guermonprez, retired in 1968.

The firm was set up in 1938 when Guermonprez left Cleeves Ltd, chemists and photographic suppliers of Bognor Regis, to branch out on his own. He employed two photographers, each on a starting salary (in 1946) of £2.10s; he also covered many events himself, particularly social and official gatherings. He was a perfectionist in and out of the darkroom, often working from 8.00am to 8.00pm, including Sundays. Every year he made a point of visiting Chichester's hospitals on Christmas Day to photograph the entertainments and parties laid on for patients.

For the interest of the technically-minded it is recorded that the CPS photographers used VN press cameras, which were loaded with 9 x 12cm glass plates. On a typical assignment a photographer would only take about twenty such plates and was therefore rendered considerably less mobile than today's pressmen. On returning to the firm's premises, the negatives would be developed in specially designed racks and printed on overhead Kodak enlargers. Developing and printing was an important part of the business. Bastow's, Timothy White's, and other local chemists all sent films to be developed in the firm's laboratories.

The surviving negatives cover the usual range of work undertaken by provincial photographers of the time. There are countless weddings, children's parties, football teams, works' dinners and passport photographs. The firm was often employed by local businesses to photograph their premises for advertisements and the city engineer commissioned pictures of building projects, demolitions and traffic schemes. The result is an unrivalled archive of views of Chichester's streets, of buildings long since vanished, and of shops now closed and all but forgotten.

Much of the CPS work was done for the *Chichester Observer*, which in the early post-war years did not employ a locally based photographer. Consequently, the collection includes a wide variety of newsworthy events. Harry Guermonprez ran Chichester Photographic Service until his retirement in 1968 and lived in his home in West Mead Road until his death in December 1973. We are fortunate to be able to include a very rare picture of Mr G. on the other side of the camera's lens.

In January 1997 a selection of pictures from the collection was chosen for an exhibition in the West Sussex Record Office by Steve Griffiths. Over a thousand people came to see it, many of whom could identify younger versions of themselves or members of their families. One lady was amazed to see herself as runner-up to the Ideal Girl competition at Shippam's Social Club in November 1955.

It was about this time that Chalford Publishing approached Ken Green, who has been responsible for four previous books on the subject of Chichester's past, with a view to producing a book of pictures of Chichester to be part of their Archive Photographs Series, covering most of the larger towns and cities in the country. This provided the ideal opportunity to publish some of the pictures from the collection that have not been seen since their original publication over 40 years ago.

To the pictures from the Record Office were added many from Ken Green's own collection and from that of Peter Parish. As a result we believe that we have a selection of pictures that will remind those who lived in the city at the time, and inform those who have arrived since, of two decades of change in Chichester.

We take this opportunity to thank Richard Childs, the County Archivist of West Sussex for allowing us to reproduce photographs in his care, and also Peter Parish for so unselfishly letting us take the pick of his collection.

Chalford Publishing are fast becoming known internationally for their excellent publications depicting local scenes. We hope that this volume will sit happily alongside the others in their series.

Ken Green and Steve Griffiths
Chichester, March 1998

One

Shops

If a visitor to the city, who had last seen Chichester in the 1950s and '60s, were to return today, the most striking change that he would notice would almost certainly be in the main street shops. Many old established businesses have now gone and have been succeeded by building societies, estate agents, TV hire shops and branches of the multiple stores that can be seen in any high street in the country.

It is therefore not surprising that pictures of old shops evoke vivid memories for older Cicestrians; the first selection of pictures that we show is of some of the former businesses that are no longer trading.

This picture was taken in August 1946. The lorry in the foreground still has just one headlamp, a reminder of wartime black-out regulations. Notice also Bull's emporium on the left.

West Street in August 1955, a still familiar view of passengers waiting in a queue for a bus outside the post office. Also to be seen is Gough Bros., artists' suppliers, Morants and the Tower Cafe, all now part of the Army & Navy Store.

Shoppers are seen queuing to be among the first inside Shirley's drapery store in North Street on its opening day, 11 March 1955. Shirley's was built on the site of Bull's, seen on page 9. Bargains on offer included white Turkish terry towels for 3s 11d, men's striped cotton pyjamas for 15s 11d and men's woollen underpants for 13s 6d.

This picture also shows the Southdown bus office. It closed in 1956 when the new bus station in Southgate opened.

East Street in 1954. The buildings have changed little over the years, although cars have now been banished due to the pedestrianisation of the main streets. Notice the cycles parked outside the Tudor Cafe and the delivery lorry of Henty and Constable, the Chichester brewers.

Another picture of North Street taken in the late 1950s. Take particular notice of Sidney Bastow's, the chemists shop in the centre of the photograph.

The next pictures show the inside of Bastow's and evoke the distinctive atmosphere of the premises as well as portraying the usual medicines, toiletries and baby foods associated with a chemists shop.

Bastow's were among the first to deal in photographic goods and could offer excellent advice to would-be cameramen.

Woolgar's grocery shop in The Hornet in June 1956. Cyril Woolgar sold a complete range of groceries. The building to the left was at one time a dairy. Note the three-wheel, single-headlight vehicle in the foreground.

Also in The Hornet was Allman's garage which had been a petrol station in pre-war days and had then moved into agricultural engineering. The business seen here in 1955 eventually moved to Birdham.

Charlie Hooker, tobacconist and confectioner in Westgate was a small shop, but it was known to many, particularly workers in the nearby County Hall.

Two
Demolition

Sadly, many old buildings, some of which had been landmarks for centuries, were demolished during the period covered by this book. Today we have in place legislation that should prevent such vandalism ever recurring.

First a series of pictures that show the demolition of Sharp Garland's shop in Eastgate Square in March 1964. The loss of this building, which was reputed to be the oldest grocery shop in the country, saddened most Cicestrians.

To give readers an idea of the premises' original appearance we include this photograph which was taken in 1920 when the business had just received its first motor vehicle.

The City Engineer and Surveyor, Mr Ian Wilson (second left) with members of his staff and fire officers meeting opposite Sharp Garland's shop to decide the fate of the building which had become unstable and dangerous. Incidentally, Goodridge's, the shop in whose doorway they stand, was once, in the nineteenth century, Chichester's fire station.

Demolition work commences and already the roof has gone.

Demolition took place on a Sunday as the shop was on the main bus route out of the city. This view shows the immensity of the task.

Geall's demolition contractors of Bognor Regis were kept very busy in Chichester during the 1950s.

After the shop was gone the site stood empty and overgrown for twelve years before being redeveloped.

A 1972 view of the new Lennard's shop that replaced the scene in the previous photograph. On the left is Storry's, Chichester's music shop.

Opposite: Barrett's former shop on the corner of South and West Streets was used for a while by the Festival Theatre. Later, it had to be abandoned as parts of the structure were unsafe. Finally it had to be shored up in August 1969 when its walls began to give way. Here it can be seen held up by scaffolding.

Also in 1969 on the opposite corner by the Cross, Lennard's shoe shop had started to fall apart. Once again massive timber shoring had to be put in to hold it in place until demolition could take place.

Another scene that is no longer with us. This was the 'bottleneck', a narrow stretch of road at Westgate.

The same stretch of road from the west.

The shorings go up again, this time at Penny's shop in North Street.

This picture shows the demolition in Southgate to form the Avenue de Chartres section of the ring road system.

Here, in August 1965, the road is under construction. The College of Further Education, as it was then called, can be seen in the distance.

Three
New Building

The views in the preceding section, showing buildings in the process of being demolished, make rather depressing viewing. However, there was a great deal of new construction taking place during this period. Indeed, it is doubtful whether at any time in the past so much activity has taken place to affect the appearance of Chichester as it did during the period covered by the following photographs.

This sequence of pictures were all taken on more or less the same spot in Southgate. In the first one we see the Old County Police Station which had become redundant when the new police station was built for the West Sussex Police Force in Kingsham Road in the 1930s. The building was used by the army during the war, but had lain empty until being demolished in 1954.

October 1954. Here we see the site cleared in readiness for the builders. Notice the Southgate level crossing and the Basin Road gates in the distance.

May 1955. The steel frame has now been assembled and Drewitt's, the builders, have affixed their sign. The size of the building is now becoming apparent to Chichester inhabitants.

A view from the north showing the nearly completed building. Note the gas works' gasometers in the distance. The properties on the right have since been demolished.

Finally we can see the finished building which opened for business in 1956 and has hardly changed to this day.

This photograph shows the St Richard's Roman Catholic Church which was demolished in 1958.

The congregation moved to the new church in Market Avenue, seen here being built in November 1957.

In 1960 the old White Swan Inn at Westhampnett was pulled down. In this case the new premises had been previously constructed.

In 1961 British Railways decided to pull down the old Chichester railway station and replace it. This photograph of the old building was taken just before the demolition team arrived.

Another view from the same time, taken from the pedestrian footbridge over the railway lines.

The old building comes down. The doors to the former entrance hall can be seen on the left.

The framework of the new building, together with the new footbridge, begins to take shape around the waiting passengers. In the background can be seen one of the gasometers of the Chichester Gas Works in Stockbridge Road.

The new platform canopy takes place.

The completed building. Readers will be forgiven for thinking that, with the addition of a coat of paint, it would have been better to have retained the original building; it is an opinion that was shared by Nikolaus Pevsner the celebrated architectural historian.

A building that was generally applauded by all is the County Library Headquarters and branch library in Tower Street. It was designed by Mr F.R. Steele the County Architect up to the time of his retirement in 1964 and erected under the supervision of his successor, Mr B. Peters. The engineering consultants were Messrs Ove Arup and Partners who were also responsible for the Sydney Opera House at about the same time. The first picture in May 1965 shows the foundations of the site. The difficulty for the builders in setting out such a building is very apparent, although after Sydney it must have seemed simple stuff for the engineers.

By February 1966 the pre-cast concrete framework is in position.

October 1966 and the building nears completion.

On 24 January 1967, the building was completed. John Snelling the chairman of the building company responsible for the project hands over the key to Professor Asa Briggs, the Vice Chancellor of Sussex University, for him to carry out the official opening ceremony.

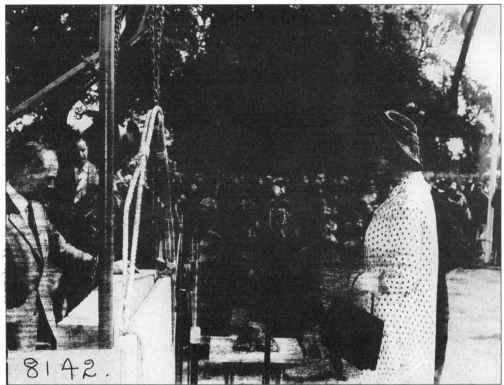

In 1961 the Chichester Festival Theatre was being constructed in Oaklands Park. The foundation stone was laid by Her Royal Highness Princess Alexandra on 12 May.

By 23 November 1961 the building was completed up to roof level. Here is the building under wraps, prior to being roofed.

February 1962. The building is complete although the surroundings have some way to go. Leslie Evershed Martin and the Mayor, Councillor John Selsby, are making an official visit. The theatre opened for its first performance on 5 July 1962.

Inside the wraps Sir Laurence Olivier joins the workmen in a toast to celebrate the 'topping out' of the building.

A more recent picture of the theatre as seen by today's theatregoers, showing the Minerva Studio Theatre extensions and the Cathedral in the background.

Four
Schools

Changes were taking place in Chichester schools. In 1944 new legislation, popularly known as The Butler Act, raised the school-leaving age to 15. This, together with a wider curriculum, immediately gave rise to problems of overcrowding. New premises were built for the Lancastrian Boys' School at Kingsham so that they could move from Orchard Street; the Lancastrian Girls expanded into the vacated buildings.

The boys moved into the new school over a period of several months. Here the first contingent are seen queuing outside a classroom in January 1955.

In this scene in April 1955, boys are assisting with the unloading of boxes and furniture supervised by Mr Lewis the headmaster.

Here the unpacking has started in the school's chemistry laboratory.

Each year a Sportsman of the Year award of a cricket bat was made at the Lancastrian Boys' School. It was known as the Voke Bat and given by Mr W.J. Voke in memory of his son who had attended the school. In 1955 it was presented by the Sussex and England cricketer, James Langridge, to 16 year old Robert Hammond, captain of football and cricket at the school. The bat had been autographed by the England and South African teams and here Robert is proudly showing it to his envious friends.

The school was officially opened on 18 April 1956 by the Dean, Walter Hussey.

A picture of pupils at the High School for Girls in the science laboratory in February 1955.

Opposite: Dame Sybil Thorndyke laid the foundation stone of the new Bishop Luffa School on 27 July 1962. It was Chichester's first Church of England Secondary School. The Bishop, Dr Roger Wilson, performed the dedication and Mr John Snelling, the builder, who we saw at the opening of the library, can also be seen here with Dame Sybil.

Another picture of the Girls' High School taken in their dining room in 1955.

The scholars get down to work at the Lancastrian Infants School in May 1956

Two charming pictures of pupils of the Lancastrian Infants School taken in May 1956, included for both the quality of the photograph and the joy shown in the children's faces

Finally in this category, pupils of the Northgate House private school visiting the mound in Priory Park.

Five

Sporting Activities

There has never been any shortage of recreational and sporting activities available for those who live in Chichester and its surrounding area. In the 1950s Goodwood, which was better known as a horse racing course, became a venue for motor racing enthusiasts. The perimeter track of Woodcote airfield, built in the war as a satellite to Tangmere RAF station, was also used for motor racing. All of the leading drivers of the time came to race here.

The first picture shows the start of a 500cc race at the Whit Monday meeting in 1955.

The race track also attracted other personalities. In June 1956, director Ralph Thomas shot scenes of a film to be called *Checkpoint* at Goodwood. The star in this scene is Anthony Steel who drove an Aston Martin in the film. He had been expected to stay at the Norfolk Hotel in Bognor Regis, which was besieged by teenage girls clutching autograph books. In fact, he stayed with his wife, Anita Eckberg, in Midhurst, where it was reported that Miss Eckberg rose at midday dressed in a pink and white candy striped shirt and tight calf length pink trousers and carrying a black woollen handbag. Unfortunately, we do not have a picture of that occasion.

The Ecurie Ecosse racing team from Scotland competed at many of the Goodwood meetings. Here, in September 1956, they are preparing a D-type Jaguar.

The start of the annual Chichester to Portsmouth road race in May 1962, which was won in record time by Bob Roath of the Walton Athletic Club.

Chichester had a regular Cricket Week every summer in the 1950s when the Sussex team usually entertained one of the university teams and the Hampshire County XI. The two batsmen striding out to play in August 1956 are Ken Suttle (left) and G.H.G. Doggart.

One can get an idea of the popularity of Cricket Week from these two photographs showing the spectators.

This picture of racegoers and bookies in Goodwood's Trundle Enclosure in 1952, with a police sergeant keeping a watchful eye over them, is a remarkable example of the photographer's skill.

The view seen by those in the preceding picture. The large building in the foreground was the members' stand; it has since been demolished to make way for the new grandstand.

Six
The Military

There has been a military presence in Chichester since the building of the barracks off Broyle Road in the early nineteenth century, when troops were accommodated in buildings originally constructed to house French prisoners. From 1873 the city became the garrison town of the Royal Sussex Regiment until it was amalgamated with the Queen's Regiment in 1977. The barracks then became the training depot of the Royal Military Police, who had had men stationed there since 1964.

The Army recruiting office for Chichester was in South Street, as seen in this 1955 photograph.

Another photograph of stunning quality; this one shows the bandsmen of the Royal Sussex leaving for Korea from Chichester railway station on 16 October 1956. They took the 10.25 to Southampton, where they embarked on the *USS Nevassa*.

National servicemen of the Royal Sussex being inspected by Major R.G. Harrison, the Commanding Officer, on their passing-out parade in November 1955.

Onlookers at Quebec Day (the barracks' open day) Sunday 16 September 1956. This was an annual event to commemorate the Royal Sussex Regiment's part in the Battle of Quebec, 1759. One of the highlights for children was a ride in the captured staff car of German General Von Armin.

An earlier picture showing soldiers of the regiment who left in August and were posted to Kohima Camp along the River Imjin under the command of the 4th US Infantry Division.

The first of the Royal Military Police 'Redcaps' arriving at the barracks in January 1964.

In August 1964, in their first year at the barracks, the RMP had an open day when over 100 veterans arrived from all over the country for Old Comrades Day. Here are two Chelsea Pensioners, both former 'Redcaps'.

We must not forget the Royal Air Force at Tangmere. They had an open day on 18 September 1954, when over 15,000 members of the public turned up. Among the attractions were fly-pasts by a Spitfire, a Tiger Moth and various modern jet aircraft. Here we see visitors queuing to be photographed in a Meteor fighter jet plane.

A gliding school opened in Tangmere in 1963 and the first person to qualify as an instructor was Flt Lieut Dennis Rogers who was the Commanding Officer of the Chichester ATC. Here he is receiving his instructor's wings from the CO of the Gliding School, Flt Lieut William Verling.

Flt Lieut Rogers seen with an ATC Cadet.

Seven
Royal Occasions

On 30 July 1956, The Queen and Prince Philip paid a visit to the city. Pictured here are the crowds waiting for the royal visitors in St Martin's Square.

Their wait is rewarded as the royal motorcade arrives in St Martin's Square where Her Majesty was to visit St Mary's Hospital.

The route was lined with what seemed to be every airman in the RAF. They were from the RAF stations at Tangmere and Thorney Island and were issued with white rifle slings and belts for the event.

The royal car proceeds along North Street.

Received in Priory Park by the Lord Lieutenant, the Duke of Norfolk, the royal party was presented to the Mayor, Leslie Evershed-Martin, Bishop Bell, the High Sheriff and others. After receiving a loyal address the Queen walked past thousands of onlookers to the Guildhall Museum, stopping to talk to groups of elderly people and schoolchildren.

The weekend before the royal visit was marked by two days of severe gales and rain which caused £1,500 worth of damage to the street decorations. In this picture the decorations are being put up on the Friday before the visit.

This view shows the decorations being repaired and replaced on the Monday after the gales.

Another royal visitor was the Queen Mother who came to Chichester in July 1965. She is pictured here at the Cathedral, where she was introduced to pupils of the Prebendal School. Later she went on to officially open Bishop Luffa School, where she asked that the pupils be given a day off to mark the event.

A reminder of the city's street decorations at the time of the Queen's Coronation in June 1953. This picture shows South Street looking towards the Cross.

Another view of the 1953 Coronation in South Street, this time from the cross.

More coronation decorations, in North Street.

Eight
Somerstown

Many writers have decried the demolition of Somerstown in 1964. This was a residential district of Chichester, built mostly during the early part of the nineteenth century, which housed what was called before the days of political correctness, working class families.

In fact Somerstown was a community of a kind that no longer exists in the city. Most of the residents were rehoused by the Council in the several housing estates being built at that time. If you speak to any one of the former residents they nearly all express a nostalgia for High Street, George Street and Cross Street, all of which made up Somerstown. The following pictures show demolition taking place.

High Street. The residents have gone and the windows are boarded up awaiting the bulldozers.

First the roofs of the houses on the corner of High Street and Cross Street are stripped of tiles.

Musk's tobacconist and sweet shop, well known in its time for giving 'tick' to the needy, also awaits its fate.

Pictured from the same viewpoint, at a time when the shops are almost gone.

This stretch of shops in Broyle Road, adjoining Somerstown, was also demolished

The lady in this photograph was 71 year old Mrs Alice Gilbert who refused to leave her two-bedroomed cottage. She was in dispute with the city council over the amount of compensation offered to her.

Here Mrs Gilbert speaks to the men who can go no further until she leaves. The sharp-eyed reader will spot a broom outside her home, which was maybe there to repel bailiffs.

Another picture of the demolition taking place.

Surely these flint-fronted cottages in George Street could have been economically restored and renovated to make very attractive properties?

The former Primitive Methodist Chapel in Broyle Road was used by Pickford's as a furniture store when this picture was taken in February 1964.

Later it was isolated by the demolition and was finally demolished in 1965.

Nine
Events

A selection of photographs taken from the Record Office collection showing events that occurred during the period covered by this book. Although some are of a minor nature they do help to build up a picture of residents' interests and activities during the post-war period in Chichester.

In February 1957 Chichester became twinned with the city of Chartres in France. Here French visitors are being welcomed by Alderman Charles Newell and his wife.

It was in 1963 that excavations started on the archaeological finds at Fishbourne. This picture shows Dr Barry Cunliffe (standing right) directing a team of volunteer helpers.

Visitors come to view the amazing finds revealed by the excavations.

Excavating seems to have been fashionable in 1966. Here in February archaeologists defy the cold to dig in a site on the corner of St John's Street and East Street. They unearthed a burial ground belonging to the medieval Blackfriars' Priory.

In August 1963 there was another dig, this time in the land off Little London, now a car park. In the background is St Andrew's Church.

Bidding for pigs at the Fat Stock Society Show at Chichester Market on 14 December 1962.

Showing off the first prize sheep at the show.

The prize bull at the annual show was bought by the owners of Charlie Howard's, the Chichester butchers, for sale in their shop in North Street.

The cattle auction taking place in the bull ring.

Onlookers and dancers watching the May Queen procession, May 1963

Members of the Portfield Bonfire Society making torches for the Guy Fawkes celebrations in Chichester on 27 October 1956. Two hundred people, members of Bonfire Societies from Beeding, Littlehampton, Patching and Chichester, formed a procession through the city to the bonfire in Florence Road Playing Field.

The band of the Welsh Guards marching along North Street on Chichester Gala Day in July 1956. The band headed a mile long procession of carnival floats through the city.

The 1963 May Queen, 15 year old Jean Street, being paraded through South Street in a Triumph Herald, followed by the dancers seen in the earlier picture.

The undoubted highlight of the July 1962 Gala were the Dagenham Girl Pipers (whatever happened to them?). Here they round the Cross in a morning demonstration before the afternoon's carnival.

The cornflower was adopted as the emblem for the city's Gala days. Here, on 14 July 1956, three *Observer* journalists, Gordon Morris, Mervyn Curtis and Paddy Welch, are seen purchasing their flowers from a seller wearing Elizabethan costume.

Opposite: One of the entrants in the 1956 Gala procession was the Chichester Girls' Club demonstrating their sporting activities.

The Pilferington Report, winner of the best float in the 1962 Gala procession, entered by Percy King, the Chichester builder; it satirised the recently published Pilkington report on television.

The Liberal Party float in 1962.

A vigil being held outside the Cathedral by members of the Campaign for Nuclear Disarmament in April 1963.

Schoolboys enjoying themselves at the Civil Defence Exhibition in the Assembly Rooms, September 1954.

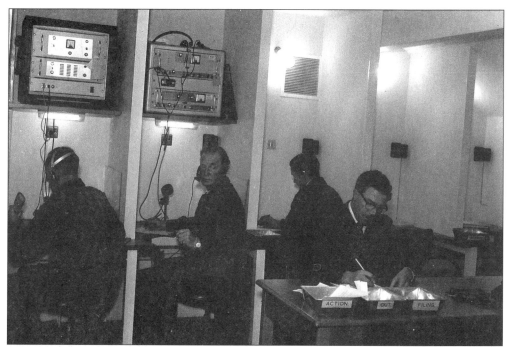

West Sussex County Council built a new civil defence centre underneath the council chamber of County Hall in 1962. It had a one foot thick concrete roof and was designed to control operations in the event of a war or natural disaster.

Guests waiting to be announced at a reception held by Mayor Selsby in Priory Park, June 1962. The event was to enable the great and good of Chichester to meet actors and actresses from the Festival Theatre shortly before its official opening. More than 500 attended, including Sir Laurence Olivier, Sir Michael Redgrave and Dame Sybil Thorndyke. Waiting to be announced is theatre critic Bernard Levin.

The Mayor, John Selsby, receiving a shoe shine from members of the Chichester Boys' Club during their fund raising week in October 1962.

Two photographs of the train crash at Barnham Station on 1 August 1962. The 10.17 Brighton to Portsmouth train collided with the eastern end of platform no. 2, overturning the two leading carriages and jamming them between the two main line platforms. Several passengers were injured and many were dragged from the wreckage by men from Hall and Company who ran from their nearby yard to help.

The line remained blocked until the following morning when normal services were resumed.

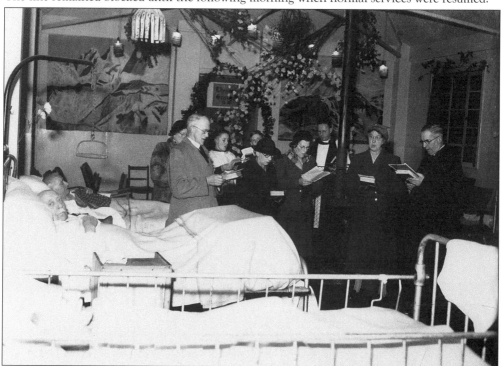

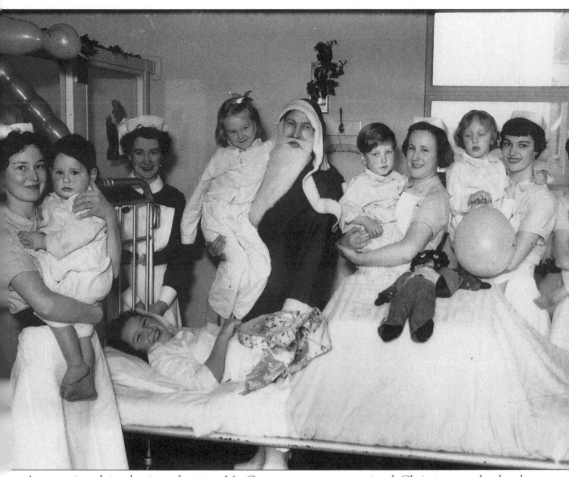

As mentioned in the introduction, Mr Guermonprez never missed Christmas at the local hospitals. We include a selection of these pictures. The first is in the children's ward of St Richard's Hospital, 1954; Father Christmas this year was one of the medical registrars.

Opposite: Carol singing in one of the hut wards at St Richard's, Christmas Eve 1954. Note the solid fuel heater around which the singers are gathered.

Christmas 1954 in the Royal West Sussex Hospital, and nurses, singing carols, are visiting each ward.

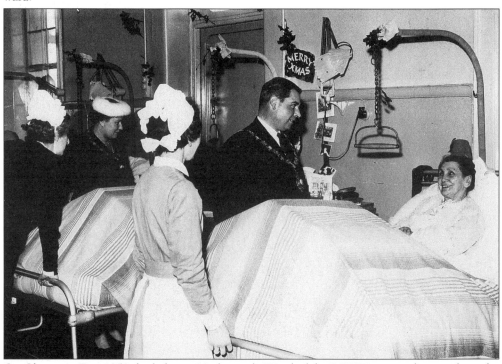

On Christmas Day 1958 the ladies in Nightingale Ward of the RWSH received a visit from the Mayor, Alderman Newell with his wife the Lady Mayoress.

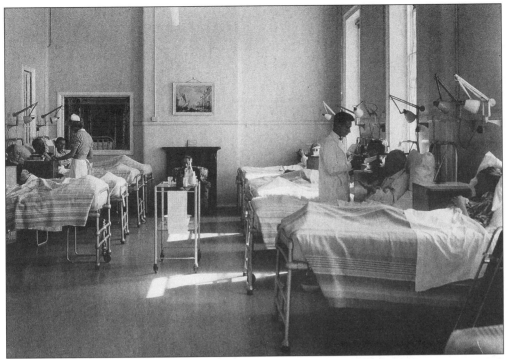

A picture of Dixon Ward, men's surgical, in the RWSH, taken in 1959.

In January 1963 the condition of the stonework on the Cathedral bell tower started to give rise to concern that it might fall on to passers-by. Pictured here are the team of four specialist steeplejacks scraping the loose stone from the surface.

This view from above gives an idea of the task facing the steeplejacks as they abseiled down the building.

This stonemason is removing the parapet to the bell tower before replacing it with new stone.

Merrymakers dancing around the Cross, New Year's Eve 1955.

A newspaper vendor in East Street, November 1955. We have not been able to find out any information concerning the intriguing headline.

Contestants in Chichester's Ideal Girl contest on 24 November 1955. Fifteen girls took part, all between the ages of 14 and 26, held at Shippam's Club. The judges looked at the girls as they sat at tables drinking tea, eating biscuits and listening to music. An assessment was made of each contestant's hair style, complexion, charm, voice and figure. The winner was 16 year old Margaret Smith, now Mrs Barrett, from Orchard Street, seen here second from left.

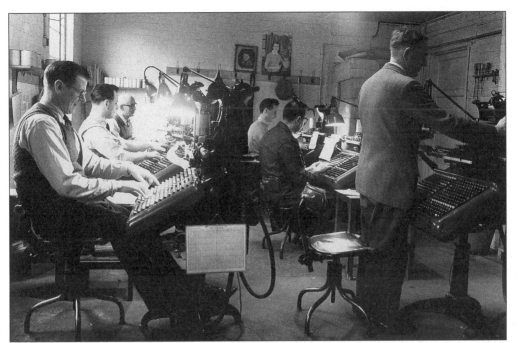

An interior view at Acford's printers in Terminus Road Industrial Estate in March 1957, demonstrating skills now swept away by computerisation.

The strange gyrations of these ladies can be explained: they are members of Marks and Spencer's staff learning the new dancing craze known as the twist.

In 1955 the Chichester Registry Office was in East Street, opposite what is now MacDonald's restaurant. This picture in February of that year shows Sir Ronald Gunter, a former racing motorist and racehorse owner of Aldwick Bay arriving, with his bride, for his fourth marriage. His bride, Mrs Phyllis Wallace, had been married twice previously. Before the war Sir Ronald had set a speedboat record from Dover to Calais in the vessel *Miss Bognor Regis*. Since 1954 he had owned the Tithe Barn Club at Aldwick where the new Lady Gunter worked as a hostess.

A performance of *A Streetcar named Desire* at the Assembly Rooms by the Chichester Players, November 1961. The male and female leads were played by John Turner and Pearl Goodman.

The 1995 flooding of Chichester was not the first time that The Hornet had been under water. Late in the evening of 29 June 1953, the city experienced a fierce 45 minute downpour, followed by an even fiercer summer storm at 8.00am the following morning. As surface drains blocked, knee-deep floods appeared at Shippam's factory. Whyke Road and The Hornet were under water, as were the Lancastrian Boys' School and the High School for Girls, where 50 girls stayed to sit their GCE examinations.

Also taken in The Hornet, this scene shows cyclists braving the flooding. In the distance can be seen one of Cover's vehicles with a chicken shed aboard.

As a reminder, a recent picture showing the 1995 floods from much the same viewpoint as the picture on page 93.

Mothers with prams look warily at the rising Lavant Course from Green Lane Bridge in 1966.

The funeral of Dean Duncan Jones, 22 January 1955.

Dean Hussey walking in procession at the memorial service to Bishop Bell held in October 1958.

The Mayor, Mr Russell Purchase and officers of the St Pancras Corporation outside the Nag's Head in St Pancras. They have just returned from taking Christmas fare to the ladies who lived in the 'Old Dears' almshouses in The Hornet, December 1962. Behind the mayor is the ubiquitous Mr John Snelling.

To give an idea of the antiquity of the custom of taking the 'Old Dears' their Christmas dinner we include a photograph taken in 1903 showing the corporation officers about the same task.

West Sussex Young Farmers in procession in West Street on Plough Sunday in January 1962.

The procession arrives with the plough, at the west door of the Cathedral where it will be blessed by the Bishop.

Children showing the Vicar of St Peter the Great, Revd C.W.F. Bennett, the gifts that they brought to the church for its harvest festival service, Sunday 10 October 1965.

Two teams, one British, one American, of ten vintage cars each arrived in Chichester in September 1954. They had travelled 850 miles from Edinburgh and stayed overnight in the city at local garages before heading off to Goodwood for final trials. Here one of the American entrants is leaving Adcock's garage in East Street.

Ten
Group Pictures

Pictures of groups of people, sports teams, business associates or whatever, are always of interest, even if we do not know any of the people shown. Maybe it is the expressions on their faces, or seeing how fashions in dress or hairstyles have changed.

The staff of Woolworth's on the roof of the store in May 1961. The manager in the centre is Mr Richmond. In this picture one can appreciate the fine view of the Cathedral from the roof.

Prizewinners at Chichester and District Cage Bird Show, November 1961.

Pupils of St Anthony's Senior School giving an indoor display of maypole dancing with their May Queen, May 1962.

The Martlett's ladies cricket team in New Park Road Recreation Ground, April 1955.

The victorious Hunston and Mundham United football team in Oaklands Park after winning the Barham Trophy by beating Littlehampton 'B' 4-2, on 31 April 1962.

Whyke Villa FC in May 1962 before their match with Yapton, which they won 7-4.

Prizewinners in Oving's 20th Annual Flower Show in July 1962. The show attracted some 200 entries and included a sports meeting for children and an evening social.

The staff of the bottling department at Henty & Constables Brewery in Westgate, taken in December 1954. Note that they are using beer crates and hop sacks to form the staging for this photograph. In the front centre is the author's father, Arthur Green, and on his right is the head brewer Mr Griffiths who, as far as we know, was not a relative of the co-author.

The Gilbertians Cricket Club in 1960 before playing a Sussex County XI. George Gilbert, the founder of the club, can be seen on the left and Alderman Charlie Newell was the umpire on the right. In the centre the team's captain, Peter Billings, had postponed his honeymoon to play in this match. His reward was the wicket of Sussex and England batsman Jim Parks, who was at that time top in the national batting averages. Peter is seen centre front row.

A group of Russian sailors in October 1955 apparently queuing to enter Covers. They were in fact on weekend leave from their warship anchored at Portsmouth, on a sightseeing tour of the Cathedral and city.

Eleven
Personalities

A photograph of Mr Evershed-Martin showing actress Margaret Rutherford round the newly built Festival Theatre. This is one of the pictures in this book that Harry Guermonprez did not take (he can be seen smiling on the right!).

Bishop Bell and his wife welcoming the new Dean of Chichester, Walter Hussey, in the gardens of the Bishops' Palace after his inauguration on 30 June 1955.

Audrey Russell was a well known BBC commentator in 1956 when she visited Chichester as part of a series of programmes introducing the new VHF radio transmissions. Here she is seen in the showrooms of Austin Storry's in North Street interviewing Roy Lewis, the headmaster of the Lancastrian Boys School, who was a keen radio enthusiast.

Opposite: One hundred and two year old Miss Locke going to vote at the polls on General Election day in May 1955.

Tom Bartlett with the last loaf baked in Shand's Bakery in Orchard Street on 23 June 1956. This was the last bakery in Chichester to use the traditional oven fired with faggots bound with hazel wands. Tom had been a baker for over 45 years and told the *Observer*: 'real bread this was'.

Richard Butler, who lived with his niece and nephew in 55 Kingsham Avenue, is visited on 8 June, his 100th birthday, by Mayor Leslie Evershed-Martin. With the Mayor is the Mayoress, Mrs Evershed-Martin. Mr Butler lost a leg at the age of eight through infant paralysis, but went on to become a good swimmer. He ran a greengrocery business from Little London for many years. His 100th birthday party was attended by his brother Henry, aged 92, sister Anne, 83, and brother-in-law Fred Harding, aged 90.

Opposite: A clock is presented to Frank Seagrave (left) at Chichester railway station on his retirement in October 1955 after 41 years service as a signalman on the railways. The presentation was made by Signals Engineers Area Assistant Mr Pollett.

Dean Walter Hussey in the grounds of the Deanery with Leonard Bernstein, the American conductor, pianist and composer, in July 1965. Dean Hussey commissioned Bernstein to write a piece of music, *The Chichester Psalms*, which was received with great acclaim world-wide.

Kenneth Childs, a local sculptor and stonemason who worked on the repair and renovation of the stonework of the Market Cross in the 1950s and '60s.

The quality of Kenneth Childs' finished work can be seen on the carving of these finials that he was working on in the previous picture.

Mrs Violet Hudson, aged 82, winner of first prize in a competition organised by Lipton's. Here she receives the prize from Sir Francis Chichester in Lipton's East Street Shop. Mrs Hudson later gave the prize, a holiday in Paris, to her daughter, who was a French teacher.

On the barracks' open day, in September 1956, Mr Charles Berriman aged 67 of North Bersted visited the Guard Room wearing the medals that he won during the First World War when he served with the Royal Sussex Regiment. He is also displaying those of his five brothers, four of whom were killed in that conflict.

Mr R. Mayne on the day of his retirement from the Southdown Bus Company in March 1955. He had worked for the company for over 35 years and had started on the horse-drawn Chichester to Bognor bus in 1920.

Mr Mayne's job as traffic control inspector in West Street involved supervising the no.53 Witterings bus when it turned and reversed into West Street from Tower Street at the end of each journey. He is seen here in action.

In this picture Charlie Hooker, whose tobacco and sweet shop was shown on a previous page, is seen with Mrs Jean Robertson who worked for him for 14 years. They are with their entry for the Gala carnival procession. Charlie ran the shop from 1910 until his death in 1960, aged 69.

Twelve
Street Scenes

This archive collection is concluded with some pictures showing street scenes; most of them seem to have been taken for no particular purpose other than to provide a record of the streets, for which we must be extremely grateful.

Workmen in Market Avenue creating a new entrance to the Cattle Market in September 1954.

Pine's hardware store extended their Eastgate shop to Market Avenue, here seen in November 1953.

Tower Street in the January snowfall of 1954 made a picture postcard scene. On the right is Ebenezer Prior's wool warehouse, after which the new street known as Woolstaplers is named.

East Street, also pictured in the winter snow, January 1954.

North Street, January 1954, with the lion on the Council House looking like a snowman

April 1962, Chichester Scouts on their St George's Day March, proceeding along The Hornet. We do not know where they were going to, unless it was to St George's Church at Whyke.

Here, led by the Army cadet band, members of the uniformed youth organisations march to the Cathedral on Empire Youth Sunday, 22 May 1955.

The most up-to-date picture house in Chichester was the Gaumont, Eastgate Square, which opened in 1938. It was also the first to close. Here it is in June 1960 during its conversion to a swimming pool.

South Street on 16 March 1960. In the far distance the Church of St Richard has been demolished although not yet replaced. The building on the left was the GPO sorting office, now General Accident Property Services.

Near to the position of the previous picture (in fact the telephone box is common to both) is the Odeon Cinema. This building was constructed in 1936 with seating for 1,000 patrons. Originally known as the Plaza it was taken over by the Odeon circuit in 1939 and its name was changed in 1948. The queue here, in August 1954, was waiting to see Walt Disney's *The Living Desert*, advertised as 'His First Full-Length True-Life Adventure Film'.

These pictures are included as a reminder of what Eastgate Square looked like in the 1950s. The war memorial that was once where the roundabout is, was removed to facilitate Armistice Day ceremonies.

From the other viewpoint one can see Leng's furniture store in St Pancras and just a glimpse of the Gaumont.

This picture shows a non-event. On 27 November 1955, Chris Chattaway, the Olympic runner, was to be guest of honour at a reception in the Assembly Rooms to mark the opening of a new extension to the Boy's Club. He had been due to drive through the city in an open-topped car, but, arriving an hour late by train, he missed the drive and most of the official speeches. The crowd that had awaited him are dispersing disappointedly. It is however, a good view of the Eastgate shops.

A view of North Street taken from
an upper storey window in July 1954
showing the 54a bus from
Hambrook and the Ashlings.

From a nearby spot a white coated
and capped conductor ushers
shoppers aboard the no.60 from
Midhurst; it then went on to
Bognor Regis.

A wet day in South Street 1953, showing why pedestrianisation became necessary.

South Street showing Turnbull's drapery, closed and up for sale. A note on the back of the pictureshows that it was taken at 3.20pm, 16 May 1963.

The shop was demolished and Boots the Chemists' new store built, seen here in September 1970. It is now the TSB.

The Orchard Stores in East Street, better known to Cicestrians as Bunn's, after its owner. This is a 1960 picture of a shop that is still missed.

A ceramic mural was commissioned in April 1966 from Yvonne Hudson to be displayed on the new building, known as Sussex House, at the corner of Crane Street and North Street. Besides cranes it shows other birds common to Sussex.

Wadham's car showroom, Southgate, September 1959. These buildings have all now long gone to build offices.

Finally a picture taken in 1954 that could have been shot at any time in the twentieth century. It shows Vicar's Close within the Cathedral precinct; one hopes that it will survive untouched in the twenty-first century.